HAYLEE EXPLORES HER ROOTS !

(A DEEP DIVE INTO PRE-SLAVERY)

By: **Dre Mudaris**
Illustrator By: **Cameron Wilson**

ISBN: 9798510884128

Copyright © 2020 Children To Wealth

HAYLEE EXPLORES HER ROOTS

(A DEEP DIVE INTO PRE SLAVERY)

All rights reserved.

Reading Levels

Interest Level: K-Gr. 7   DRA Level: 24   Lexile Measure: 770L

Grade Equivalent: 3.7   Guided Reading: M

WATCH ALONG
(SCAN CODE BELOW)

"This is going to have to be the last game, fellas; Haylee is on her way home, and I know she is going to need help with her homework," Laquan says.

Beep!

"Seems like I spoke too soon; here she is now," Laquan says as he gets up from the table to open the door for Haylee as she gets off the bus.

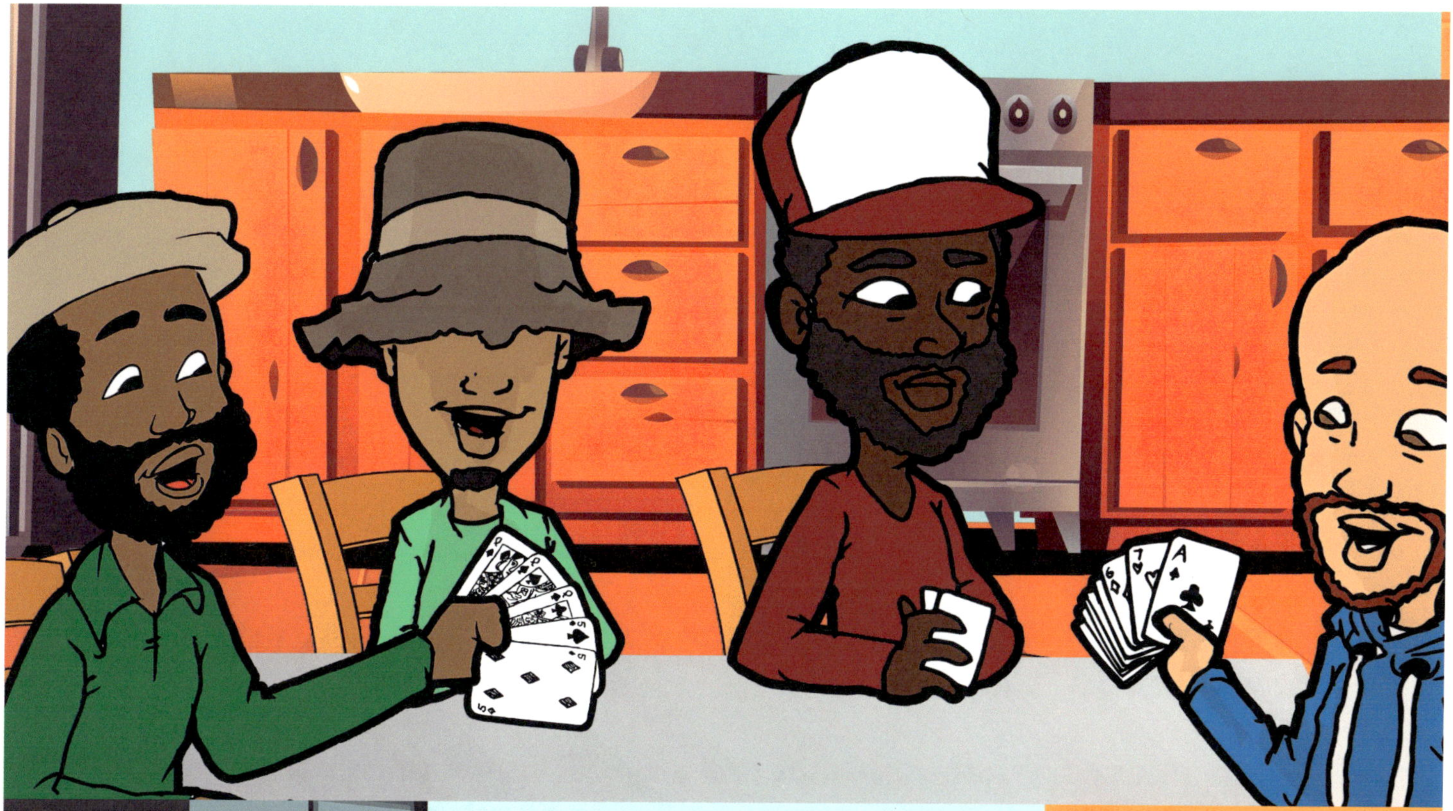

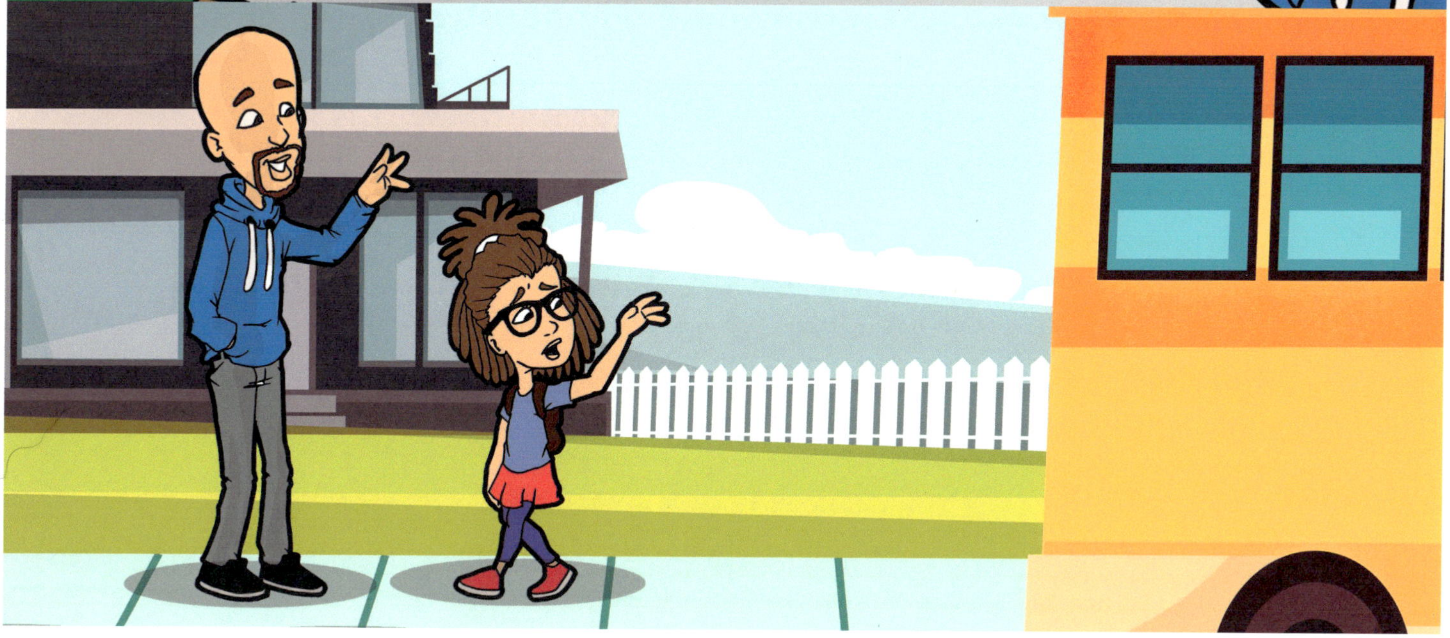

"Excuse me, young lady. Didn't I teach you manners? You know better than to not say hi to company." Laquan asks.

"Sorry, Daddy!" Haylee responds.

"Hi, Uncle Dre, Mr. Dwight, and Mr. Satiir," Haylee adds.

"Hey Princess, why the long face? " Uncle Dre asks.

"I'm just sad. We had history class today, and I'm just overwhelmed..." Haylee sighs.

Haylee pauses, then continue to say."I don't understand why our ancestors were enslaved?" Haylee begins to cry in her dad's arms.

"Aww, sweetie. It's going to be ok!" Laquan says confronting his daughter.

"No, it's not Daddy! When we went over African-American history and it seems like we began our history as enslaved people!" Haylee exclaims.

7

Laquan and the rest of the fellas look at Uncle Dre and smirk Laquan smiles and says, "I have a solution. Uncle Dre is very knowledgeable about our history as Black People. If Uncle Dre is available; I will reach out to your school and coordinate for him to come and educate your entire classroom on some facts I know will make you feel better."

"No worries, I'm in," Uncle Dre immediately responds.

"Ok, Daddy!" Haylee exclaims.

"Ok, Honey, I'll get on it. Now go upstairs and get ready to do your homework." Laquan says to Haylee.

Haylee runs upstairs

"Isn't that something? After all of these years, this "education" system still starts our history at slavery," Dwight begins to say. He continues, "As a matter of fact, I am going to help you, and we are going to make sure Uncle Dre can educate everyone on how to present properly OUR history."

"Exactly!" Laquan exclaims.

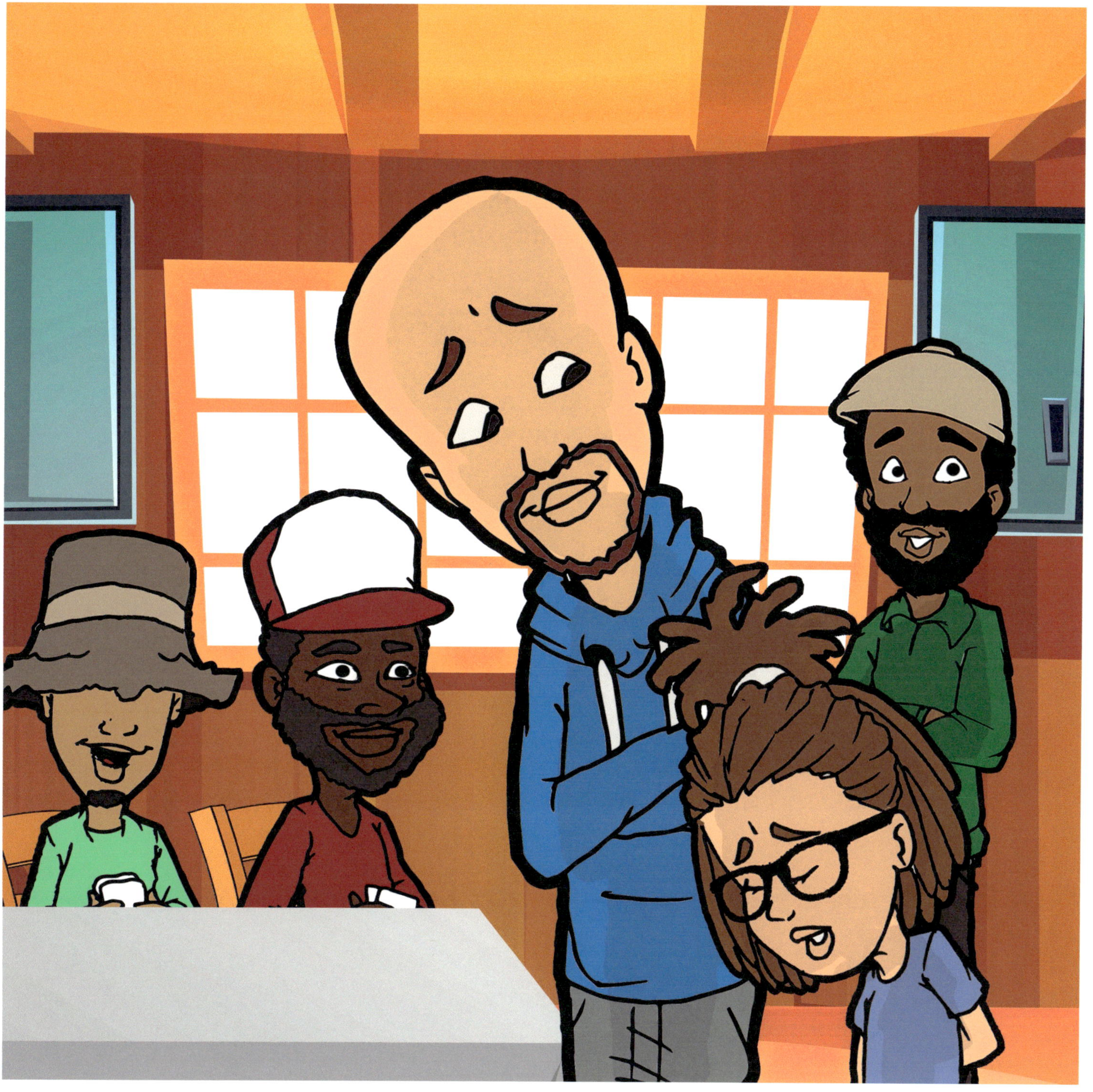

"I already emailed the principal; look, they have responded," Laquan mentions while showing all of his friends the email notification on his phone.

"The principal gave us the green light!" Laquan exclaims while reading the email. He continues, "It says here the school will be honored to have Uncle Dre come as a guest speaker, and they are familiar with all of your previous work."
"Seems like Uncle Dre has a fan," Laquan says jokingly.

They all laugh.

"Ha. Ha, very funny. No, seriously, what else did
The Principal say?"
Uncle Dre asks. Laquan continues reading, "Thank you again for reaching out. Uncle Dre coming in is perfect
timing as one of our teachers
is off tomorrow. Instead of watching a movie,
we would much rather have Uncle Dre come and speak to our children."

"Say no more. Tomorrow is perfect! Let's do it," Uncle Dre interjects.

"Well, that was quick," Satiir says.

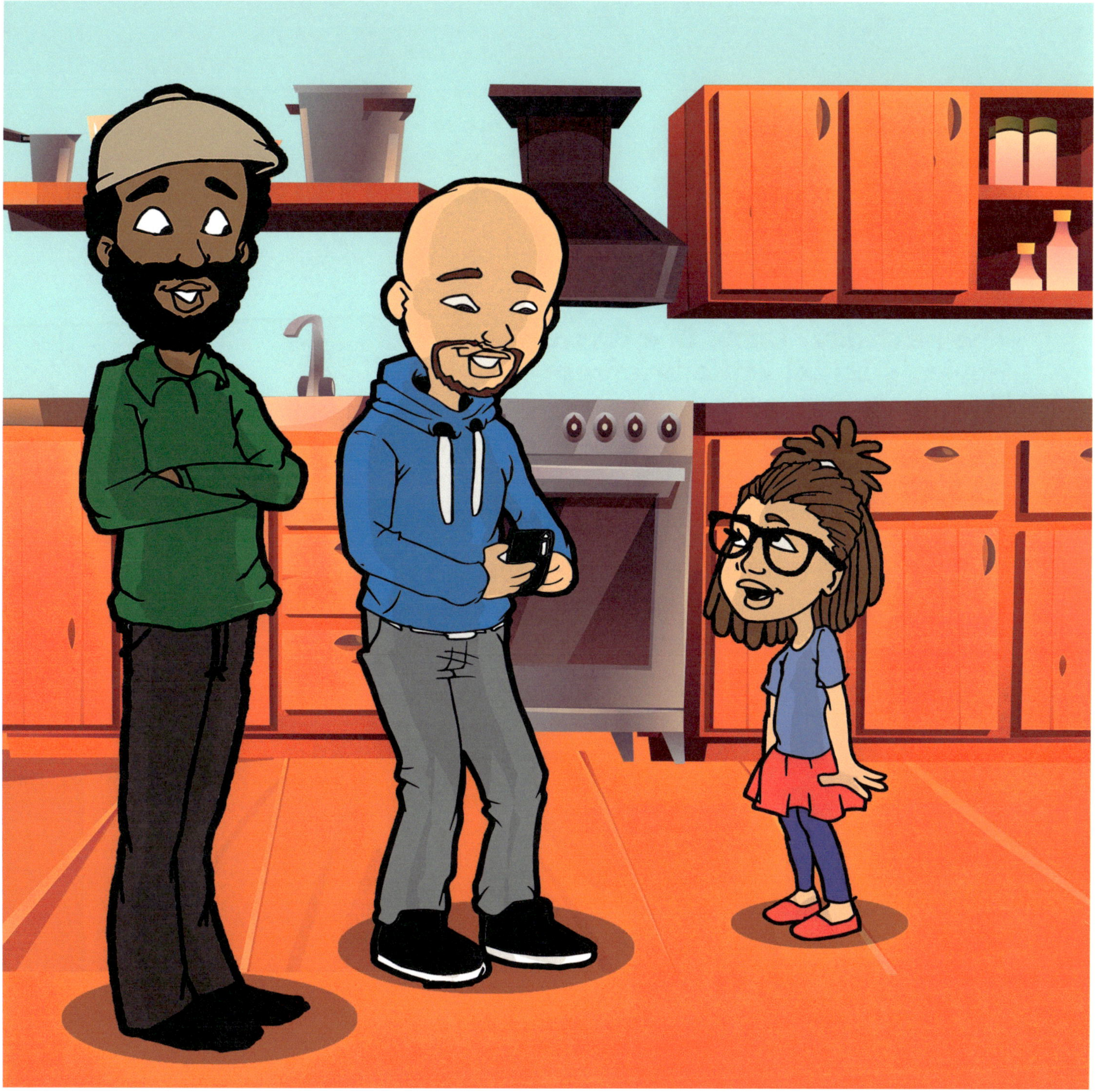

The next day, Uncle Dre arrives at
Haylee's school witha briefcase
"Hey guys and gals, we have a special guest today since Ms. Lilly is out. Everyone, let's give a warm welcome to Uncle Dre!"

The principal exclaims. The kids all clap, welcoming Uncle Dre.

"Hey, everyone!" Uncle Dre says while opening his briefcase. "Today is going to be a little different than most." Uncle Dre continues.

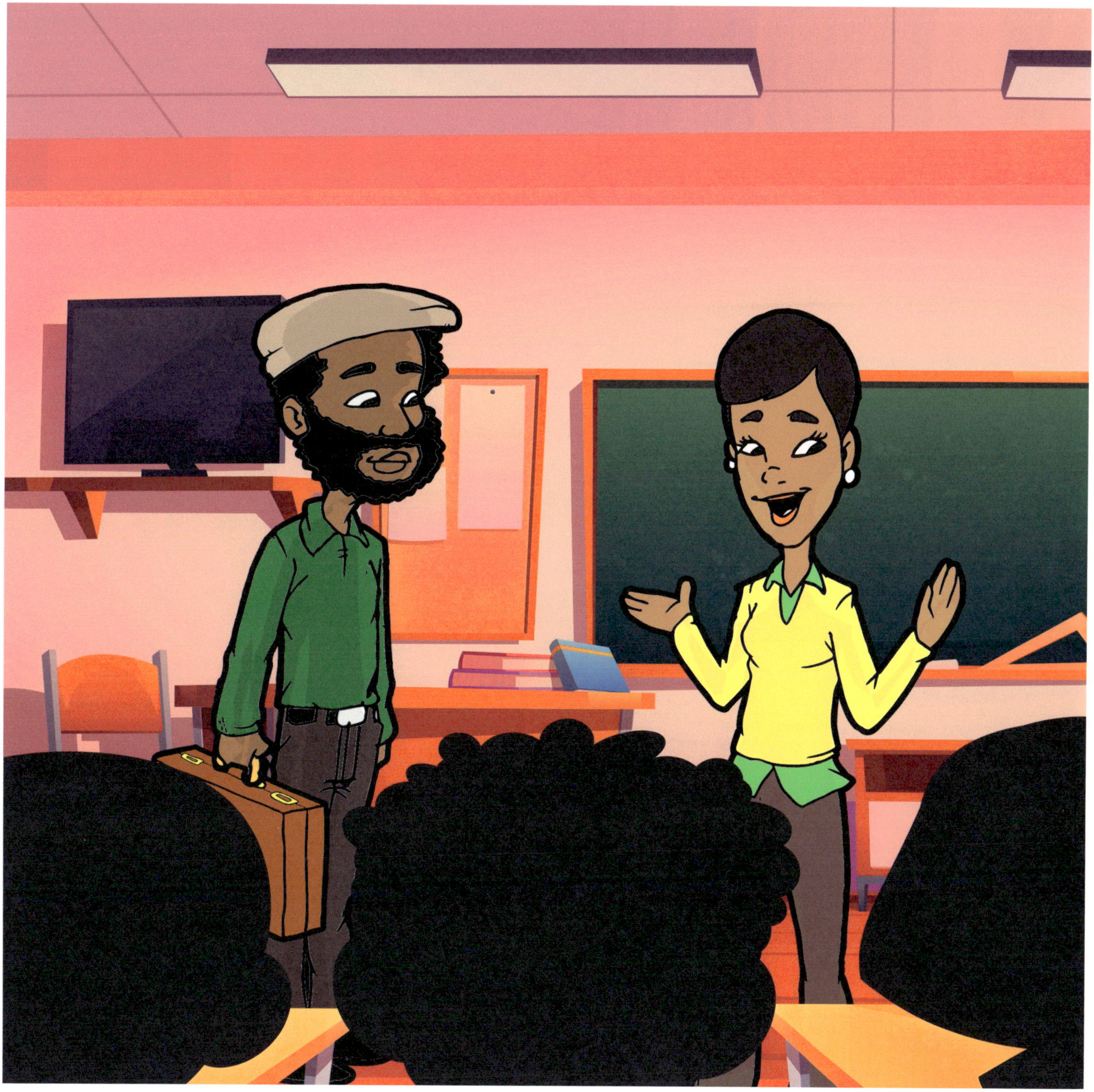

He opens his briefcase, and it extends vertically, opening up into a doorway. He then begins to instruct the kids to walk through this portable virtual door that
Uncle Dre created.

"I want everyone to stand up and get into a single file line," Uncle Dre advises.

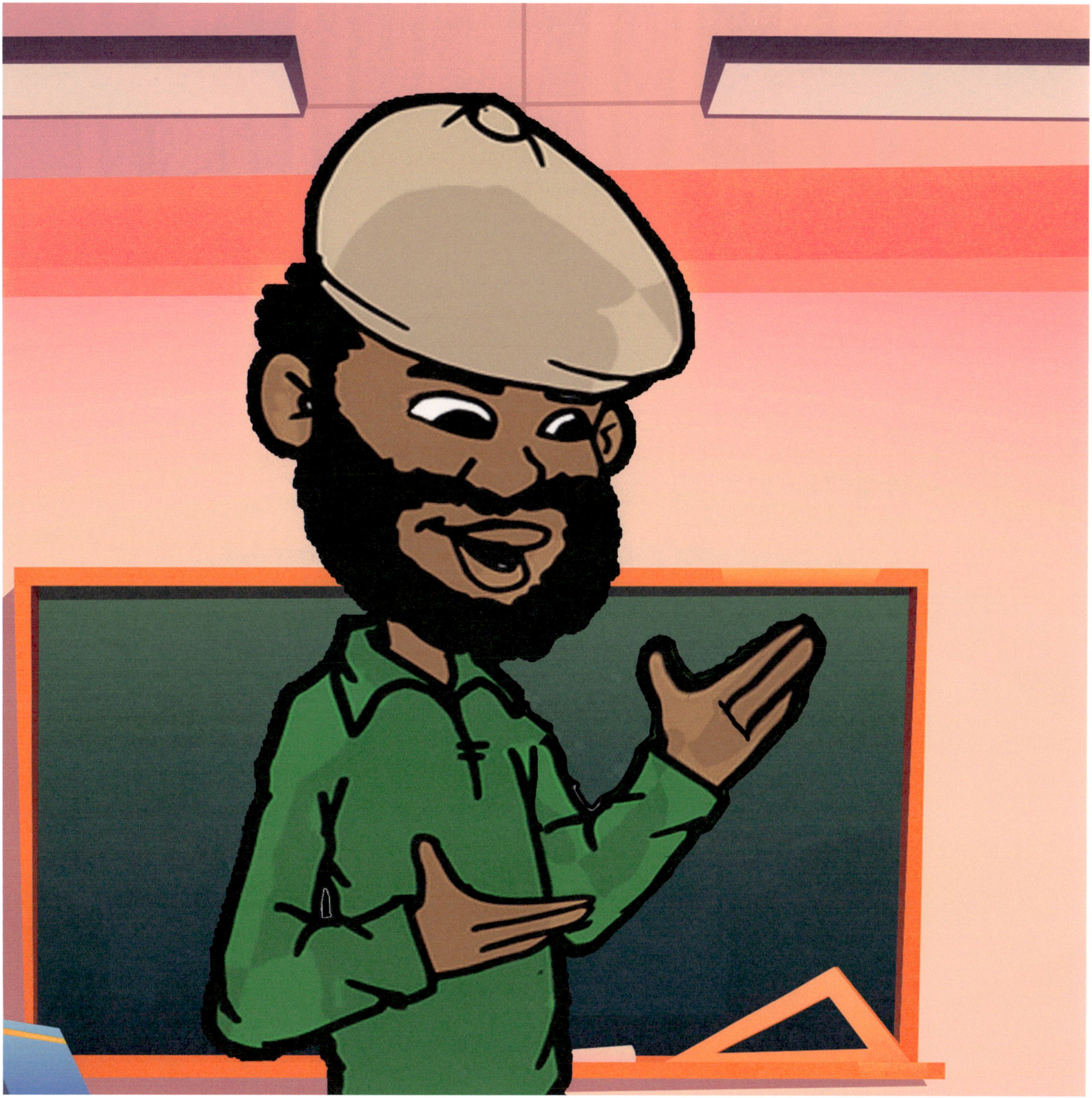

All the students walk through, and it's just Haylee and Uncle Dre left in the classroom.

"Ok, we are next. Let's go!" Uncle Dre grabs Haylee's hand and they go through the portal to meet the other students.

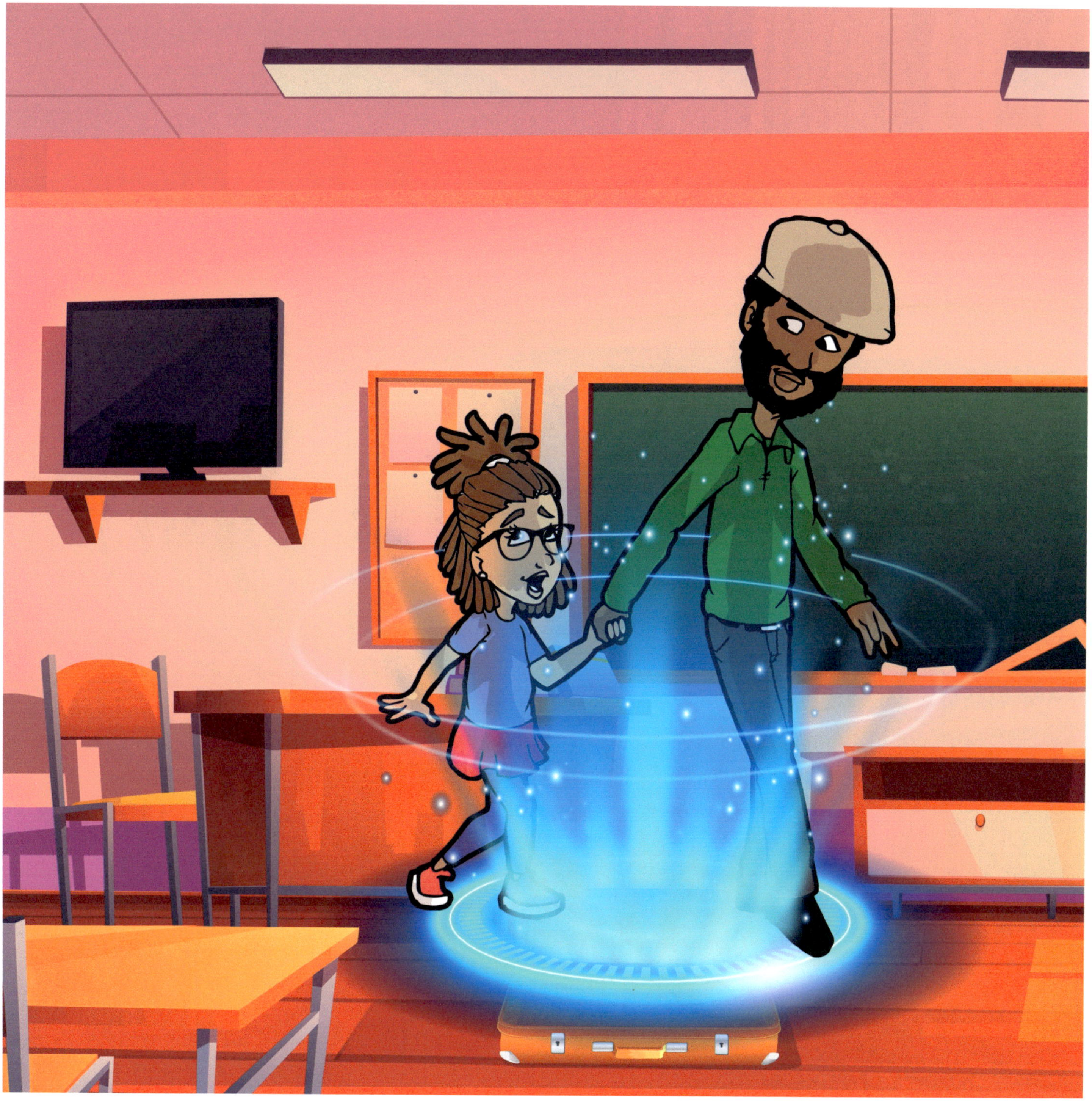

Haylee and Uncle Dre go through the portal, and they meet up with the other students who are waiting for them,
and the period is 7200 BC. (3500 years older than stone heads).

Uncle Dre and Haylee proceed to the front of the line, and Uncle Dre begins to lead the group.

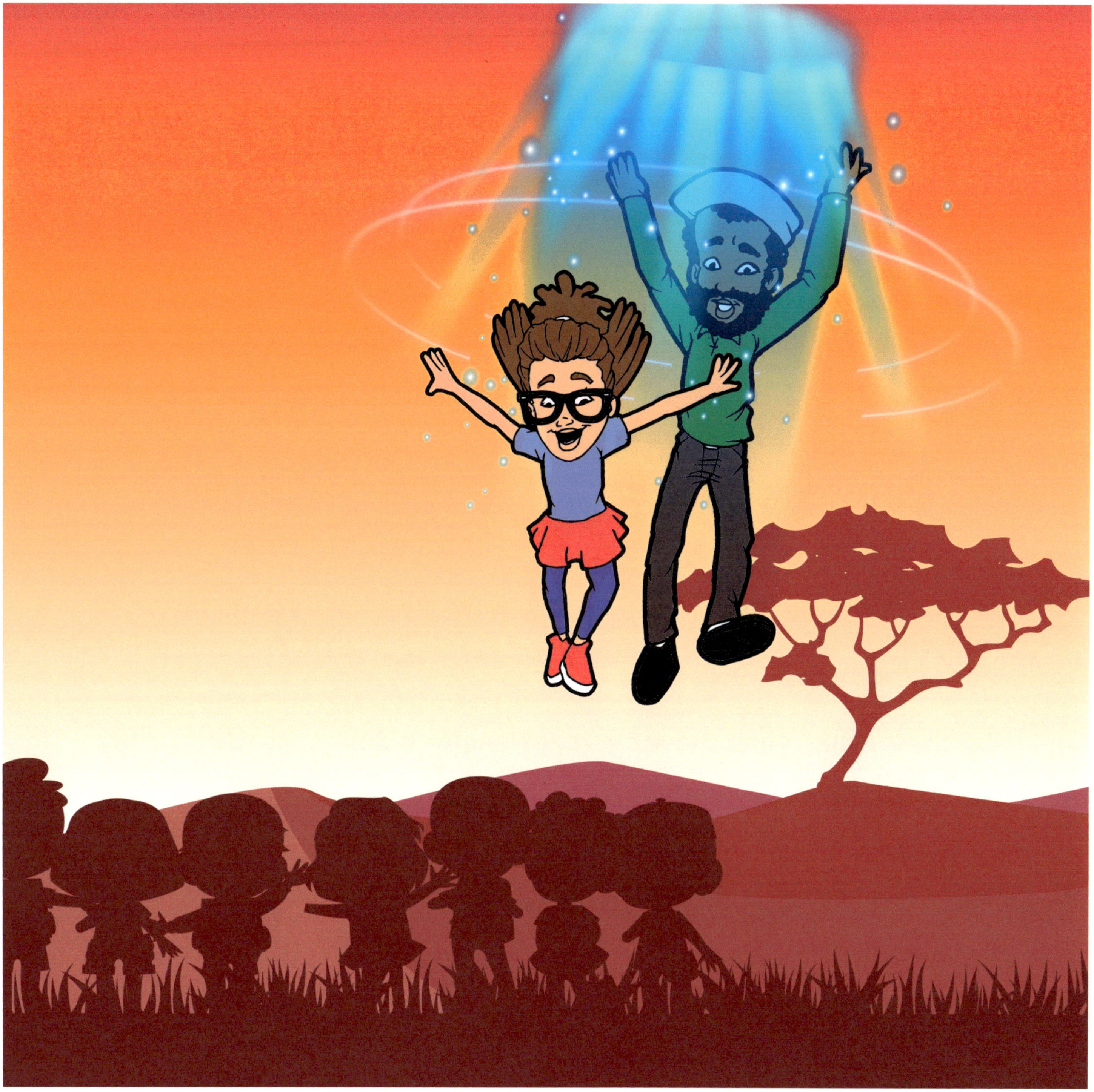

"Where are we?" Haylee asks.

"Great question!" Uncle Dre says to Haylee.

"We are in the great continent of Africa." Uncle Dre says with delight to the students.

While Uncle Dre says this. The group sees African archeologists and scientists were studying the stars.

"Hey guys and gals, follow me. I want to show you a few things." Uncle Dre says as he
leads the group.

As they walk, time moves exceptionally quickly, in which they walk through a timeline. They take a few steps, and they are in 3000 BC.

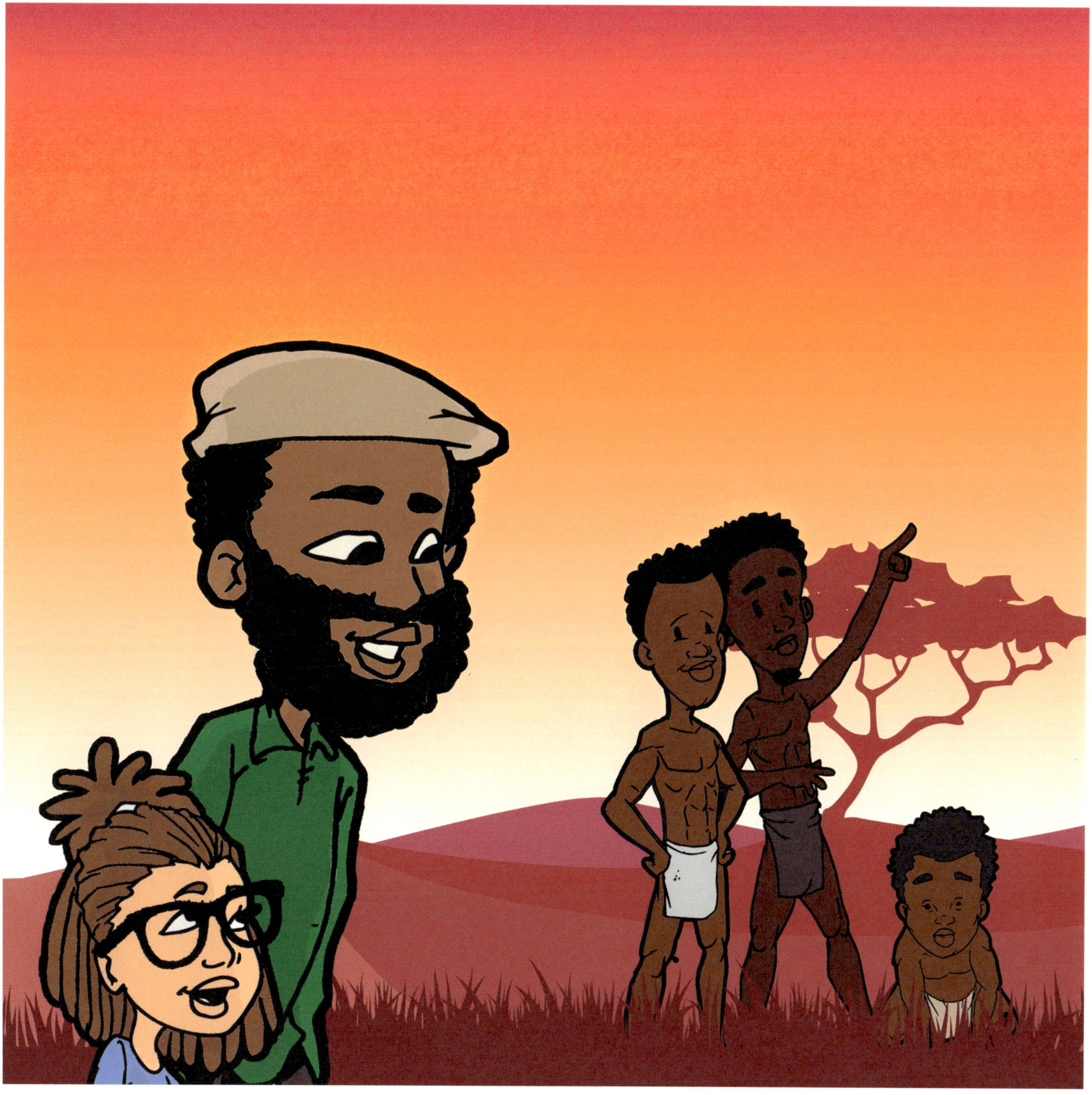

Wow, look at all these great statues," Haylee points out.
*The Students stop and are blown away by all
of the gigantic bug sculptures

"Look, they are carving one right now!" One of the students exclaims.

"Uncle Dre, what do those big sculptures represent?" Haylee asks.

"Well, Haylee, those sculptures are all our Kings and rulers. What you guys see over some men are carving an actual sculpture. They build these huge sculptures to pay respect and homage to their leadership."

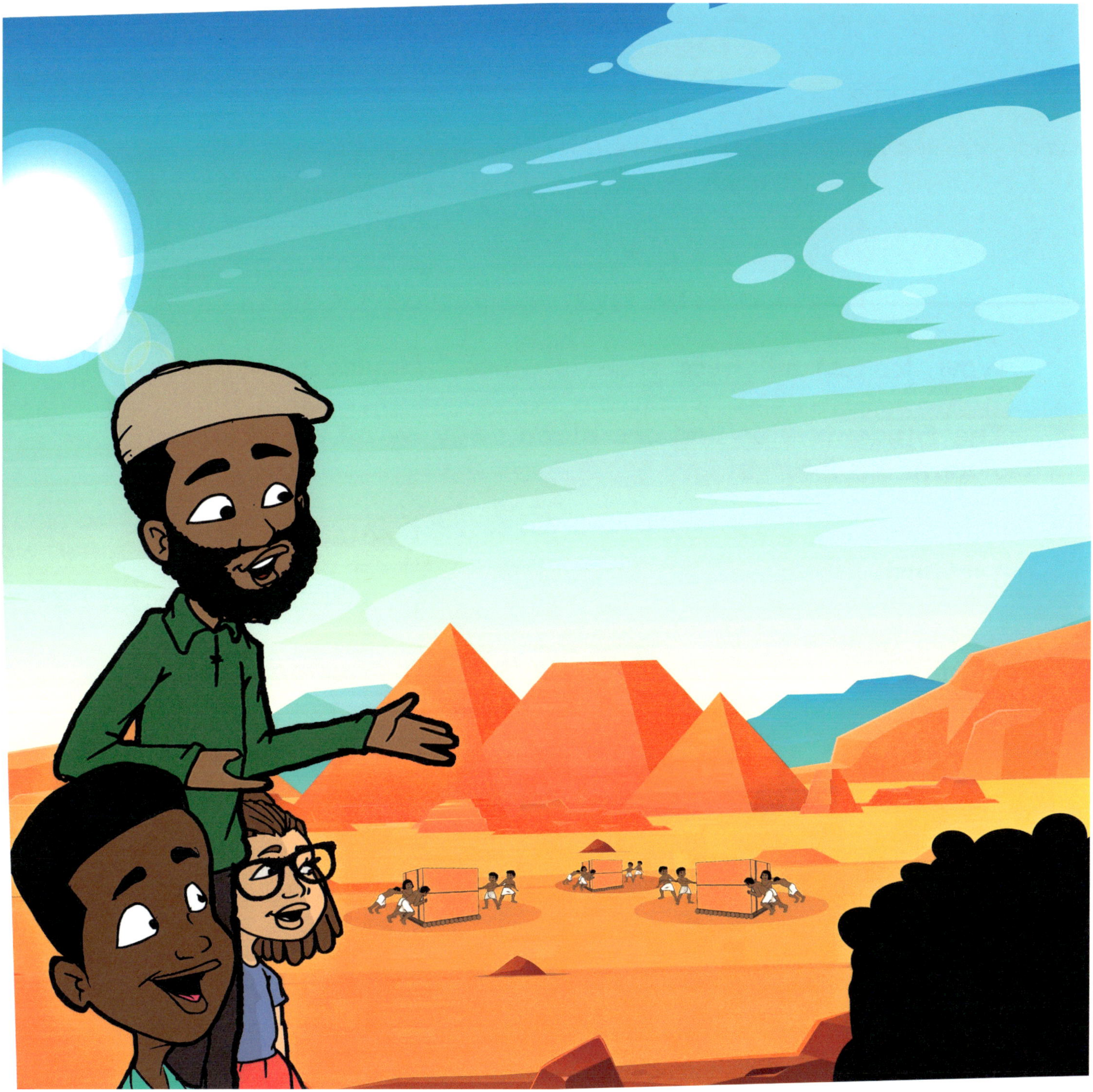

Wow, look at all these great statues," Haylee points out.

The Students stop and are blown away by all of the bugs gigantic sculptures

"Look, they are carving one right now!" One of the students exclaims.

"Uncle Dre, what do those big sculptures represent?" Haylee asks.

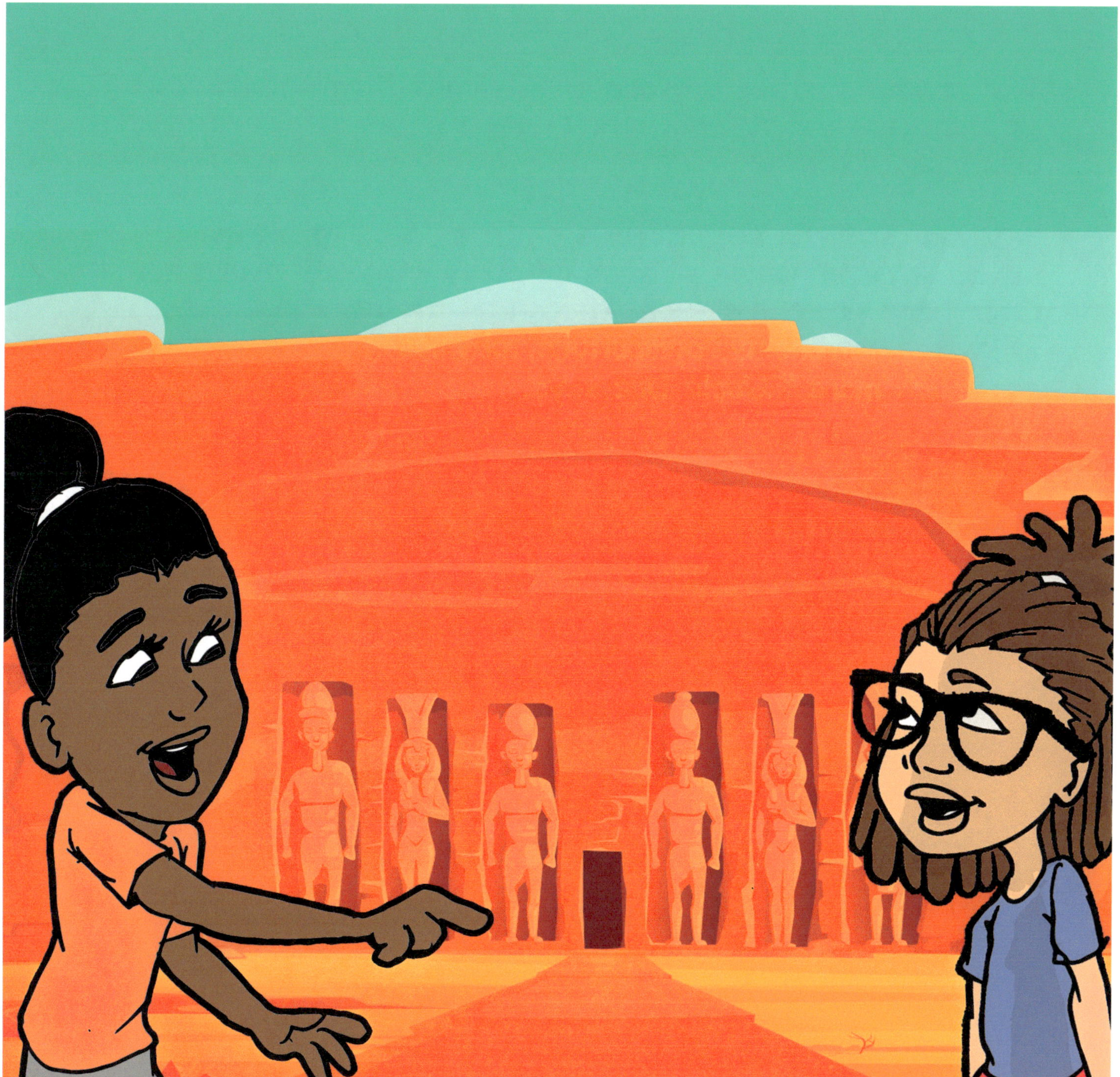

The students notice a group of Africans farming and as they continue to walk, they notice a few Africans practicing medicine.

"As you guys can see there is an abundance of richness in the African people at such an early stage of civilization. Over here you can see an African created writing, studying, astronomy, agriculture, physics, medicine, and much more," Uncle Dre says.

Imhotep- who lived in the 27th century BC, was an Egyptian polymath considered to be the **first** architect, engineer, and **physician** in recorded history. He is the first Physician to emerge, chief minister to King Djoser in the 3rd millennium bce, who designed one of the earliest pyramids, the Step Pyramid at Saqqārah, and was later regarded as the Egyptian god of medicine and identified with the Greek god Asclepius.

832 BC is when Homer wrote the Iliad and the Odyssey (The first European book was written thousands of years after Africans have been writing books).

They walk into 753 BC and they can see Romulus and Remus finding the city of Rome.

Egyptian Calendar- a civil calendar - was a solar calendar with a 365-day year. The year consisted of three seasons of 120 days each, plus an intercalary month of five epagomenal days treated as outside of the year. Each season was divided into four months of 30 days. These twelve months were initially numbered within each season but came to also be known by the names of their principal festivals. A tablet from the reign of the First Dynasty pharaoh Djer (c. 3000 bc) was once thought to indicate that the Egyptians had already established a link between the heliacal rising of Sirius (Ancient Egyptian.)

They continue to walk, and they walk into 189 AD.

"If you guys look over there, we will begin to see the first three African Popes," UncleDre says.
"There was an African Pope?" One of the students asks in disbelief.

"Yes! The Catholic Church in Africa refers to parts of the Catholic Church in the various countries in the continent of Africa. Many influential members of the early

Church was from Africa, including Mark the Evangelist, Origen, Tertullian, Saint Augustine of Hippo (from Hippo Regius in what is now Annaba, Algeria) and Clement of Alexandria." Uncle Dre answers.

"Wow!" Haylee says shockingly.

"How did the Popes come about? " She immediately asks.

"Well, Haylee, Churches in eastern North Africa, such as those in Egypt and Ethiopia tended to align with the the practice of Eastern Christianity, but those to the West generally were more Western in practice.

"Well Haylee, those sculptures are all of our Kings and rulers. What you guys see over there are some men carving an actual sculpture. They build these huge sculptures to pay respect and homage to their leadership."

"They look like me. Look! They are African Kings!" One student says in excitement.

Three early popes were from the Roman Africa Province. These were Pope Victor I (reigned c. 189 to 199), Pope Miltiades (reigned 311 to 314) and Pope Gelasius I (492 to 496); all three were North African men." Uncle Dre answers.

They continue to walk into 622 AD, where they notice people taking on a journey from a distance

"What's going over there?" Haylee asks.

"Over there is what was called the Hegira, which means Departure," Uncle Dre responds.

He continues, "This is the migration or journey of the Islamic prophet Muhammad and his followers from Mecca to Yathrib, later renamed by him Medina. This was also often identified with the start of the Islamic calendar, which was set to 16 July 622 in the Julian calendar or 19 July 622 in the Gregorian calendar."

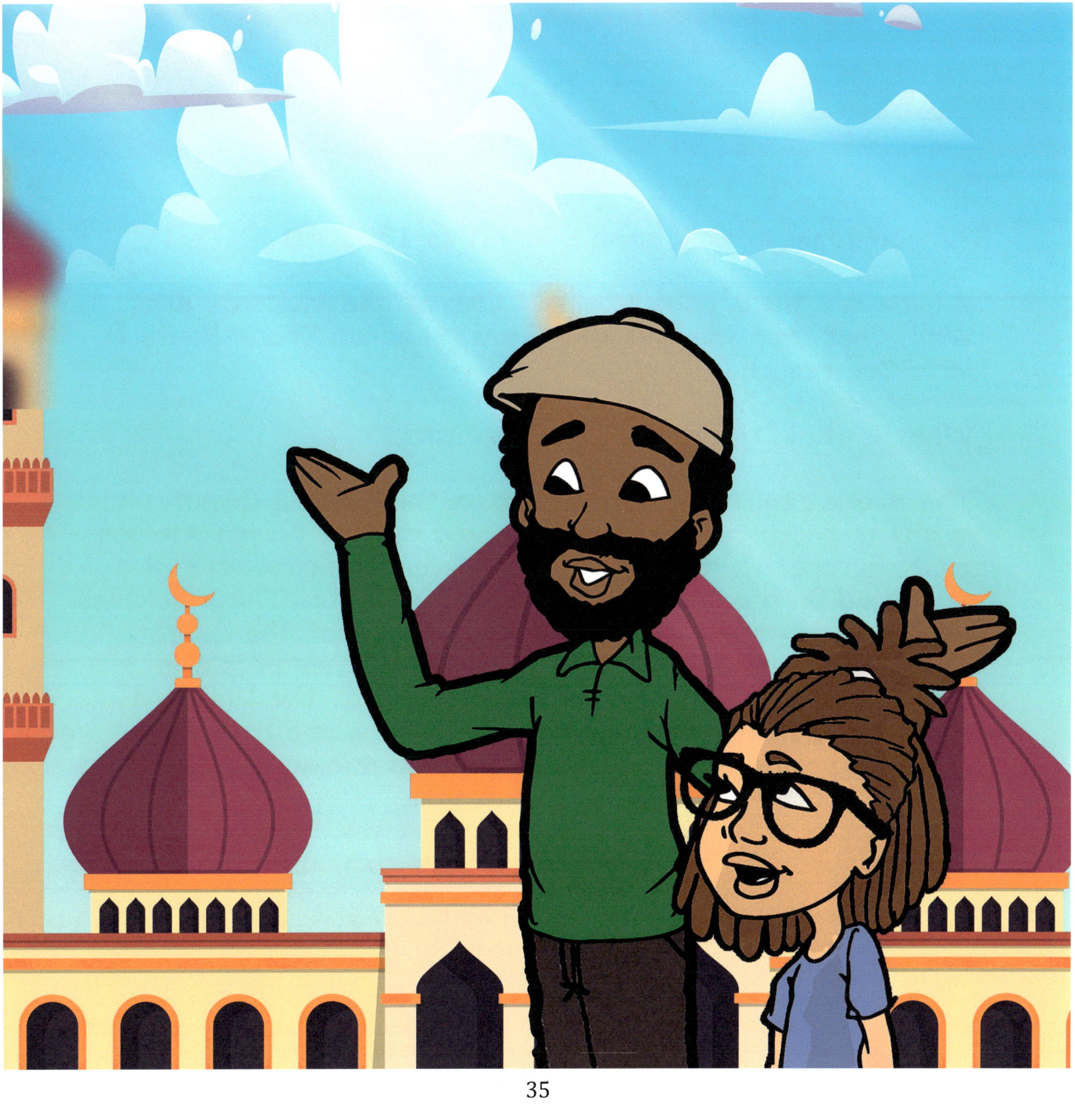

They continue to walk from 800 AD to 1300 AD.

"Where are those people going?" One of the students asks.
"Well, that over there is the Trans-Saharan Trade Route." Uncle Dre responds.

"What is that, Uncle Dre?" Haylee asks.

"This trade required to travel across the Sahara (North and South) to reach sub-Saharan Africa from the North African coast, Europe, to the Levant. Culture and religion were also exchanged on the Trans-Saharan Trade Route. These colonies eventually adopted the language and religion of the country," Uncle Dre responds. He adds, "Like some other people in Africa, During the Muslim control of some of the Western In African nations during this time, there was a non-Muslim tax and many people converted so they would not have to pay that tax and also for the enslaved Christians."

"Was this like the slave trade?" One student asks.

"There was a Trans-Saharan Slave trade, and it was the trade in "human commodity," sourced from different places in sub-Saharan Africa, destined for locations north of the Sahara Desert, the Mediterranean shores, and the Middle East." Uncle Dre responds.

Musa I or Mansa Musa-the 14th Century ruler of Mali, he may have been the largest producer of gold in the world, and Mansa Musa has been considered one of the richest people in history with an indescribable wealth. Mansa Musa conquered 24 cities, along with their surrounding districts.

Mansa Musa made his pilgrimage between 1324 and 1325. His procession reportedly included 60,000 men, all wearing brocade and Persian silk, including 12,000 slaves, who each carried 1.8 kg (4 lb) of gold bars, and heralds dressed in silks, who bore gold staffs, organized horses, and handled bags. Mansa Musa provided all necessities for the procession, feeding the entire company of men and animals. Those animals included 80 camels which each carried 23-136 kg (50-300 lb) of gold dust. Mansa Musa gave the gold to the poor he met along his route. Mansa Musa not only gave to the cities he passed on the way to Mecca, including Cairo and Medina, but also traded gold for souvenirs. It was reported that he built a mosque every Friday.

Mansa Musa's journey was documented by several eyewitnesses along his route, who were in awe of his wealth and extensive procession, and records exist in a variety of sources, including journals, oral accounts, and histories.

They walk into 1440 AD, and they hear a loud bell ring "What's that, Uncle Dre? "Haylee asks.

"That's our 5-minute mark, and the ending school's bell is about to ring. We've been out all day. Let's head back," Uncle Dre says and begins to open the portal.

Uncle Dre leads the students through the portal, and they arrive back into the classroom.

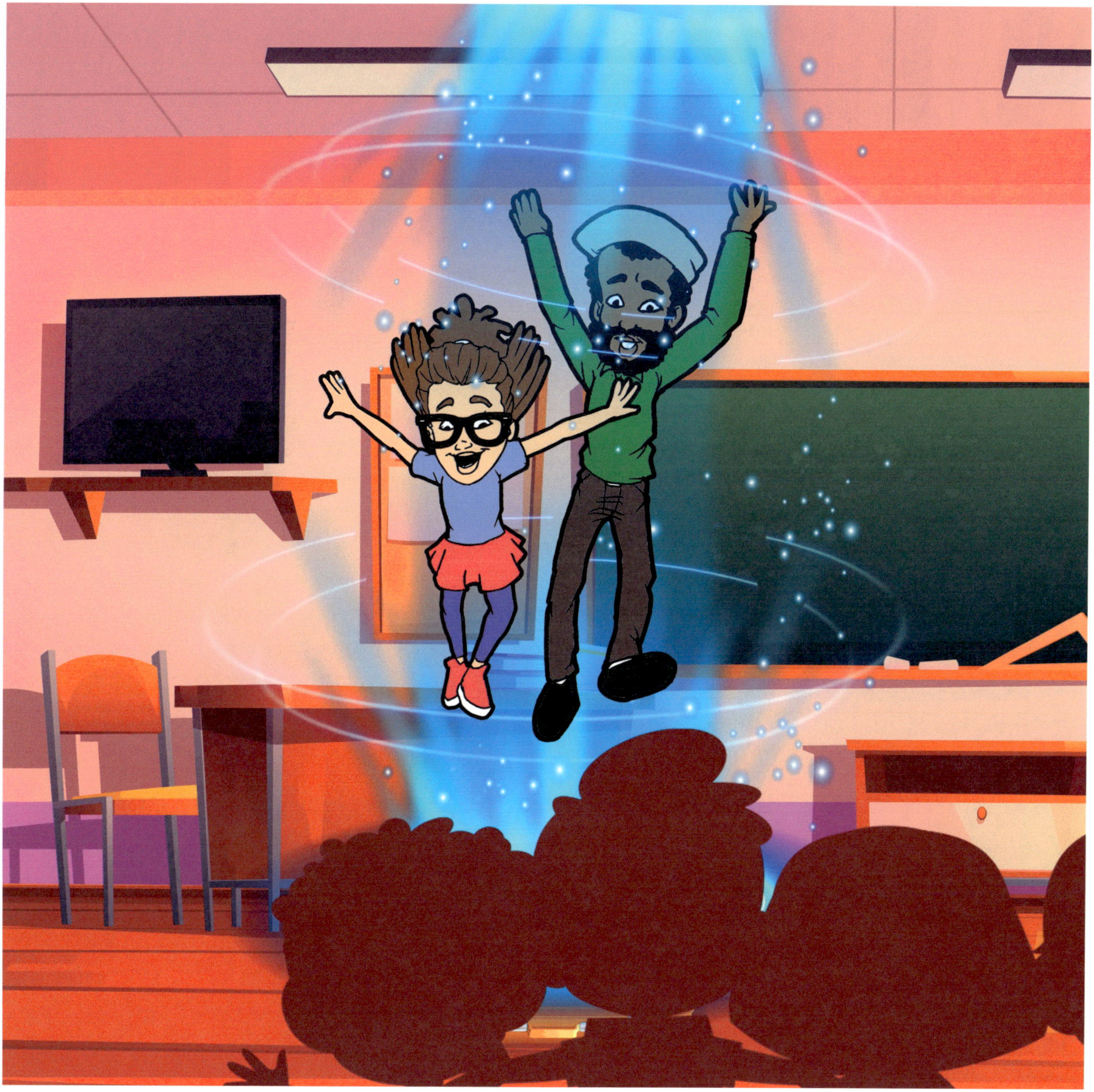

"Whoa, that was amazing!" The students exclaim.

"So much rich history! Wow, Uncle Dre!"- Haylee exclaims proudly.

"Yes, oh yeah, we left off in 1444 AD. From 1444 AD to 1880 AD was when Europeans enslaved Africans. The moral of the day, I wanted to make sure you guys and gals understand that our history pre-dates slavery, and when you think this way, you are missing out on all of the documented histories and documented success, some of which we saw today." Uncle Dre concludes.

The Bell Rings and the students don't run out of the room as usual instead, they clap and cheer for Uncle Dre, demonstrating their appreciation.

Uncle Dre closes up his briefcase and proceeds to leave the school.

The END

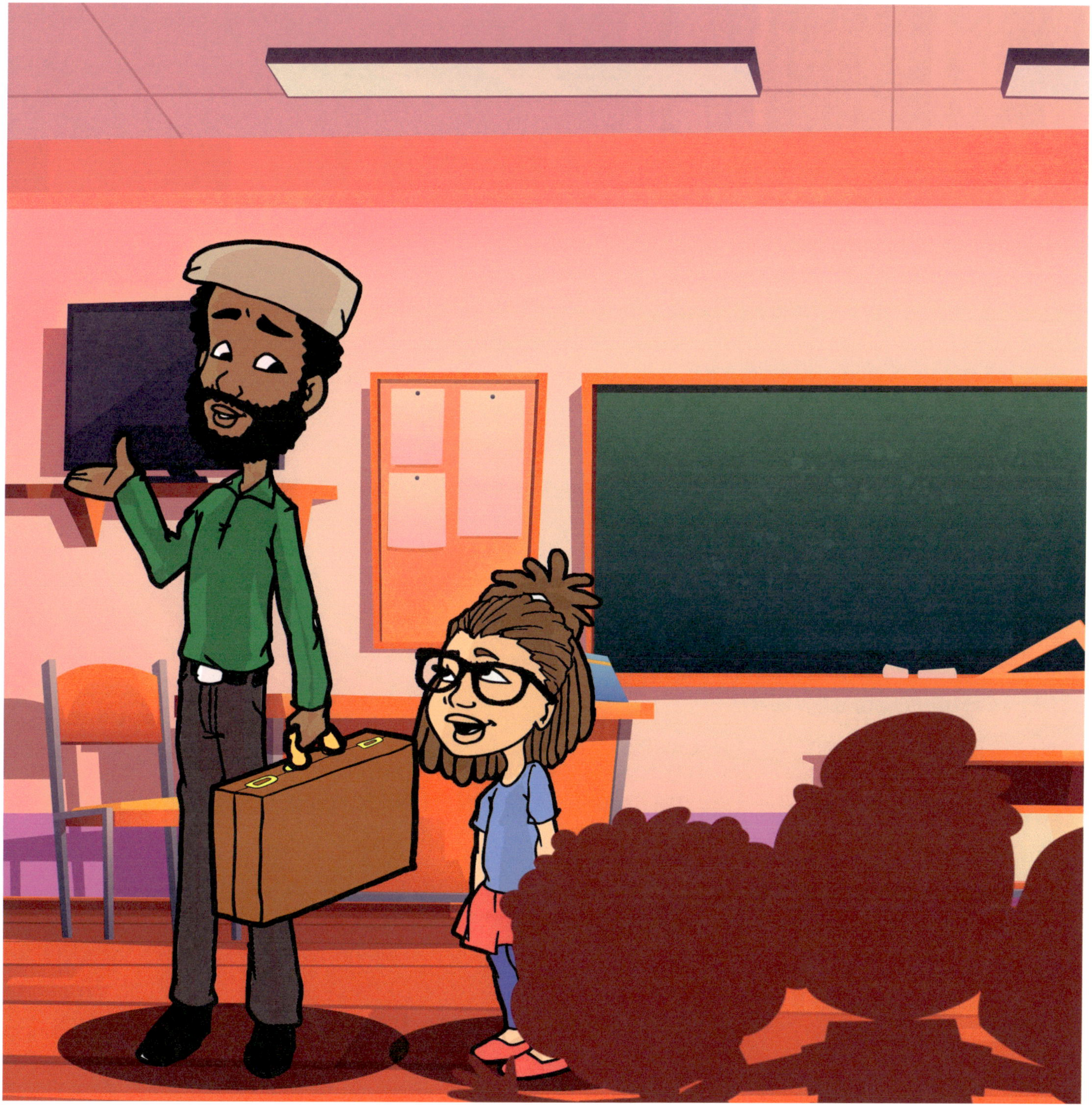

References

Meredith, M. (2006): *The Fate of Africa: A History of Fifty Years of Independence.* New York City, NY: Public Affairs.

Reader, J (1999): *Africa: A Biography of the Continent.* Nashville, TN: Vintage

Achebe, C. (1994): *Things Fall Apart.* New York City, NY: Anchor Books.

Cook, M. (1989): *The African Origin of Civilization: Myth or Reality.* New York City, NY: Lawrence Hill Books.

Mandela, N. (1995): *Long Walk to Freedom.* South Africa: Bay Back Books.

Williams, C. (1992): *Destruction of Black Civilization: Great Issues of a Race from 4500B.C to 2000 A.D.* New York City, NY: Third World Press.

Sertima, I. (2003): *They Came Before Columbus: The African Presence in Ancient America.* New York City, NY: Random House Trade Paperbacks.

Hurston, Z. (2018): *Barracoon: The Story of the Last "Black Cargo".* New York City, NY: HarperCollins Publishers.

Wilkinson, T. (2010): *The Rise and Fall of Ancient Egypt: The History of a Civilization from 3000 B.C to Cleopatra.* New York City, NY: Bloomsbury Publishing PLC.

Terms of Use

All use of the *Haylee Explores her Roots book*, accessible at www.childrentowealth.com and related subdomains (collectively, the "Web site") is subject to the following terms and conditions and our Privacy Policy all of which are deemed a part of and included within these terms and conditions (collectively, the "Terms"). By accessing the book you are acknowledging that you have read, understand, and agree to be bound by these Terms.

These Terms represent a binding contract between you and *Mudaris LLC* (and any of their respective principals, officers, shareholders, members, employees or agents are herein collectively referred to as *"Children To Wealth"* or "we"). These Terms are in addition to any other agreements between you and Mudaris LLC. If you do not agree with any of these terms and conditions, please do not use this book.

Mudaris LLC reserves the right to change, modify, add or remove portions of these Terms at any time for any reason. Such changes shall be effective immediately upon posting. You acknowledge by accessing our book after we have posted changes to this Agreement that you are agreeing to these Terms as modified.

TRADEMARKS, COPYRIGHTS AND OTHER INTELLECTUAL PROPERTY

The content contained in the book is owned, licensed or otherwise lawfully used by *Mudaris LLC* and is protected by applicable copyrights, trademarks, service marks, and/or other intellectual property rights. Mudaris LLC hereby grants you access to its original content pursuant to a Creative Commons Attribution-Noncommercial-ShareAlike License, the terms of which are accessible at: http://creativecommons.org/licenses/by-nc-sa/3.0/legalcode. *Mudaris LLC* hereby expressly reserves all rights not expressly granted in and to the book and its content.

Visit ChildrenToWealth.com and view more books that you will Enjoy!

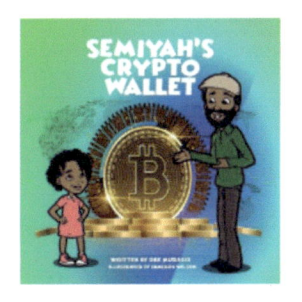

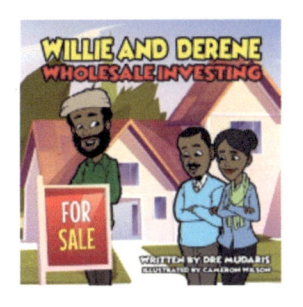

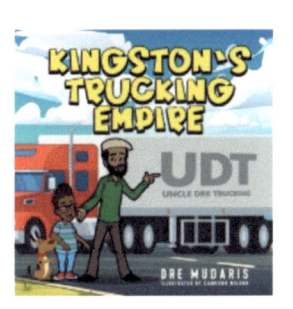

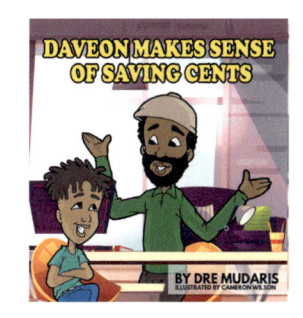

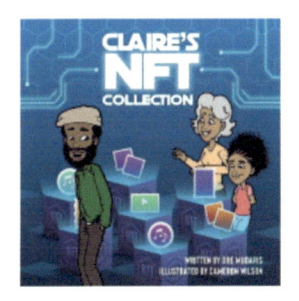

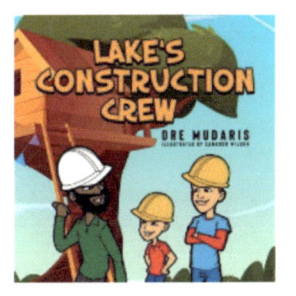

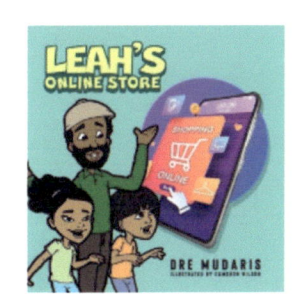

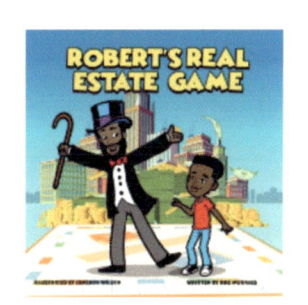

- Semiyah's Crypto Wallet
- Willie and Derene Wholesale Investing
- Kingston's Trucking Empire
- Daveon Makes Sense of Saving Cents
- Claire's NFT Collection
- Lake's Construction Crew
- Chase and Noah's STEM Program
- Kessai Fixes Credit
- Timmy Learns Taxes
- Christopher Charts the Market
- Leah's Online Store
- Robert's Real Estate Game

And Much More !!!

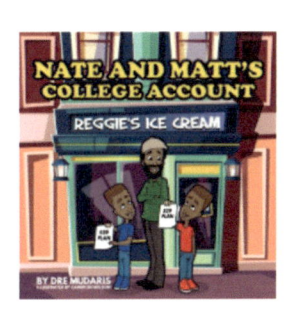

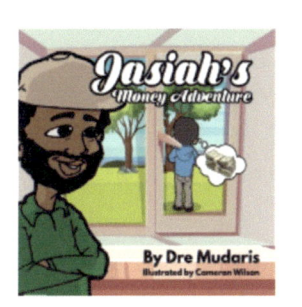

- Tor's Option Strategy
- Mary's Mental Re-Charge
- Nate and Matt's College Account
- Jasiah's Money Adventure

Made in the USA
Columbia, SC
12 August 2024